This book is dedicated to my Grandma Golda, to whom I owe
my love of tea and so much more. When she said, "It's tea time,"
I knew I was in for a treat. A wonderful cup of tea in her prettiest teacups
and goodies to eat, while sitting and talking at the kitchen table.
Those times I will remember most fondly

Designed by Roni Akmon
Written by Nancy Akmon

Cover Illustration by Harrison Fisher. Cover Design by Roni Akmon
Certain illustrations in this book are printed with permission of the Mary Evans Picture Library
and the Fine Art Photographic Library. The illustrations are by Harold Piffard, Harrison Fisher,
Kate Greenaway, William Oliver, and Howard Chandler Christy.
Efforts have been made to find the copyright holders of material used in this publication.
We apologize for any omissions or errors and will be pleased to include the appropriate
acknowledgements in future editions.

ISBN# 1-884807-46-1

Blushing Rose Publishing
P. O. Box 2238
San Anselmo, Ca. 94979
www.blushingrose.com

Printed in China

Tea Time

Designed By Roni Akmon
Written By Nancy Akmon

Blushing Rose Publishing
San Anselmo, California

The Pleasures of Tea

TEA TIME TRADITIONS

The tradition of having Tea is one of life's most wonderful pleasures. It is an elegant ritual which pays tribute to the satisfying combination of sociability and tastes. Each simple yet delectable treat, from savory to sweet, is presented on fine china and served with the perfect pot of fine tea.

The table setting can skillfully provide your guests with an elegant atmosphere which is both warm and inviting. One can achieve this by using their finest china, silver and linens. The setting is always complimented by fresh flowers. The Tea can be formal or with a theme, but always the idea is to convey a soothing atmosphere which invites conversation.

Taking time for tea, whether it's for two or for a party, is a time for reflection, conversation, enjoyment, and a release from the stress of everyday life. It is to indulge oneself in delicious bites of delicate finger sandwiches like a Stilton, Walnut and Pear, followed by a Cinnamon Current Cream Scone with jam and clotted cream, and finishing with confections such as Chocolate Dipped Strawberries and a Lemon Fruit Tart. Each satisfying bite is followed by a sip of wonderful tea, the perfect compliment.

The Afternoon Tea was brought about by the Duchess of Bedford. In the late nineteenth century, it was customary to serve dinner rather late, leaving a large gap between meals by the late afternoon. The Duchess started taking a pot of tea with light refreshments each afternoon. She invited friends to join her, and soon it became a fashionable custom. They used elegant china with fine lace and linens , and beautiful silver tea services. With the delicious array of light foods served, the Afternoon Tea became a special occasion. No matter how ambitious your plans are, we hope that you will find *Tea Time* the perfect guide to giving a most memorable Tea.

How to Prepare Tea

THE PERFECT POT OF TEA

1. First fill the tea kettle with cold water . Do not use warm water as the brewed tea will not have enough oxygen in the water and will tend to have a dull appearance.

2. Warm a clean teapot by filling it with hot water. Allow the water to stay in the pot for a few minutes. Swirl it around and pour out the water. A warm tea pot helps keep the water hot so the tea will brew properly.

3. Place in the teapot, one teaspoon of tea leaves (or one tea bag) per cup of tea and one extra "for the pot".

4. Allow the water to come to a boil. Pour the boiling water immediately over the tea, in the teapot. If the water has not first come to a boil or the temperature drops even slightly before adding to the teapot, the brewed tea will be weak and tasteless.

5. Put the lid on the teapot. Let the tea brew for three to five minutes. It is best to time this on the clock and not to judge by the color of the tea.

6. If making tea for a large party it would be wise to have two tea pots. When the tea is finished and more is needed, empty the teapot of the used leaves or tea bags and use fresh tea and boiling water brewed in the above manner.

7. When the tea is ready, use a silver tea strainer positioned over the tea cup and pour the tea. If using tea bags it is not necessary to use a tea strainer. Serve the tea with either milk or slices of lemon. A sugar bowl should be placed on the table along with silver tongs, if it is cube sugar or a spoon if it is granulated sugar.

Types of Tea

BLACK TEAS

Black Tea is a tea which has been completely oxidized or "fermented." It undergoes a two step process. First the tea is dried until the leaves are oxidized and turn to a copper color. The leaves are then put into hot air chambers where they get blasts of very hot air. This turns the leaves black in color. Black tea is a hearty, rich brew which is higher in caffeine than oolong or green tea but still contains far less than coffee. Most types of black teas are usually drunk with milk, with the exception of Lapsang Souchong and Earl Grey. Following are some of the more well known teas and blends.

Assam: This tea is grown in Northeast India. It is a full bodied tea, strong in flavor. It is a good early morning tea.

Ceylon: Grown at high altitude in Sri Lanka, it is considered one of the best teas in the world. It is strong, rich, and light golden in color.

China Black: A quality blend of black leaf teas. It has a distinctive aroma, and a smoky taste.

Darjeeling: This tea is from the foothills of the Himalayas, and is often called the "champagne of teas". It is expensive and is usually used in blends.

Earl Grey: A blend of Chinese and Indian teas, scented with oil of Bergamont. It was named after the Second Earl Grey who was given the recipe while on a diplomatic mission to China in the nineteenth century.

English Breakfast: A blend of teas from Ceylon and India. It is a full bodied, strong tea, which is best with milk. It is a popular breakfast tea as the name implies.

Types of Tea

BLACK TEAS (CONTINUED)

Keemun: A fine light colored tea, which has a flowery aroma. This tea is grown in the Anhui Province of China.

Lapsang Souchong: A popular afternoon tea, with a characteristic smoky aroma. This tea is to be served with lemon slices if preferred, but not with milk. The finest quality is grown in the Fujian Province in China.

Prince of Wales: A rich tea of golden color. It is a blend of Keemun teas.

OOLONG TEAS

Oolong teas are processed similar to black teas, but go through a shorter oxidation time. The color and taste as well as caffeine content are halfway between that of black tea and green tea.

Formosa Oolong: A tea of amber color, produced in Indochina. It has a pleasant fragrance and delicate taste.

Mainland Oolong: Has an aromatic fragrance of flowers. It is light in color and is usually scented with jasmine or gardenia blossoms.

GREEN TEA

Green teas are the most delicate in flavor of all teas. The leaves are steamed to prevent fermentation. It is naturally low in caffeine, and is best enjoyed plain without lemon, milk or sugar. There are many types of fine green teas available.

Gunpowder: This tea is from the Zhejiang Province of China. It produces a straw colored tea with a delicate taste.

Types of Tea

HERBAL TEAS

Herbal teas are know as infusions or tisanes. They can be made with a single herb, or in combination with other herbs, berries, flowers and spices. These teas are naturally caffeine free and are soothing and relaxing to drink. Traditionally, herbal teas were used as medicine. They can be beneficial in a variety of ways, such as helping you to sleep, or can be used as digestive, or some herbals are said to even ease headaches, aches and pains. It is important to remember that herbal teas should be taken in moderation, with a limit of no more than two or three cups per day. Herbal teas can be brewed as the instructions explain on page 5, or they can be brewed for medicinal purposes up to 15 minutes, for a stronger infusion. Here is a list of some delicious herbal teas and some herbal blends.

Chamomile	Rosemary
Elder flower	Sage
Fennel	Lemon Balm and Chamomile
Ginger	Mint and Ginger
Hibiscus	Mint and Chamomile
Lemongrass	Red and Black Raspberry
Marjoram	Rosehips and Hibiscus
Mint	Rosemary and Hibiscus
Rosehips	Rosemary and Lavender

SETTING THE TABLE FOR TEA

Always use your best tablecloth and linen napkins for the Afternoon Tea. Your tea service can be made of fine china or for a more formal effect, silver. Use your prettiest fine china teacups and saucers. Each person should have a small luncheon or salad size china plate to hold the various courses of tea sandwiches, scones,

Setting the Table

and sweets. The napkins should be folded nicely. Teaspoons should be placed near the teacups and saucers. Resting across each guests' individual serving plate, should be a butter knife. Set out a sugar bowl with tongs or sugar spoon, a plate of thinly cut lemon slices, and a creamer filled with milk. Have silver or porcelain tea strainers available on the table. If you are using tea bags rather than loose tea, the strainer would not be necessary.

The table can be arranged so that the guests can serve themselves, or that the hostess may pour the tea and serve each guest. The addition of fresh flowers always adds a beautiful touch. You can set the mood with some nice background music of your choice.

Each of the courses should be placed onto the table, all at once. Arrange the Tea Sandwiches attractively upon the platter or tray. It makes an even prettier presentation if you first place a lace doily onto the platter, before arranging the tea sandwiches and other courses. The scones can be arranged in the same manner on its own serving platter. Place one or two types of jam into serving bowls for the table. Clotted cream or butter should also be placed onto the table to accompany the scones. Also arrange the desserts onto a serving tray and place a silver cake server nearby.

Once your guests have arrived bring out the pots of tea or silver tea service with the delicious freshly brewed tea. Serve and enjoy!

Tea Sandwiches
&
Savories

Goat Cheese & Watercress Tea Sandwiches

INGREDIENTS

6 oz. soft French goat cheese , room temperature
1/2 cup washed and chopped watercress leaves
8 slices whole wheat sandwich bread
4 tablespoons butter, room temperature
3/4 cup finely chopped toasted pecans
Garnish, watercress sprigs

INSTRUCTIONS

1. Chop the pecans in a food processor. Put the chopped nuts onto a plate and reserve.

2. Mix together the goat cheese and chopped watercress in a bowl. Season with salt and pepper.

3. Spread the bread slices with butter. Cover half the slices with the goat cheese mixture. Press the other slices of bread on top. Trim off the crusts. Cut each sandwich diagonally in half (like an x), to form 4 triangles.

4. Lightly butter the edges of the sandwiches and dip each edge into the chopped pecans. Garnish with watercress sprigs.

5. Arrange the triangles onto a platter. The tea sandwiches may be made up to 2 hours ahead, if they are covered tightly and refrigerated.

Chutney & Cheddar Tea Sandwiches

INGREDIENTS

1/3 cup Major Grey's Chutney
1/2 pound grated sharp Cheddar cheese
1/3 cup sour cream
3 oz. cream cheese, softened
Salt and Pepper
8 thin slices sandwich whole-wheat bread
4 tablespoons butter
1 teaspoon medium curry powder
1/3 teaspoon lemon juice
3 tablespoons mayonnaise
1/3 cup chopped fresh coriander leaves

INSTRUCTIONS

1. In the bowl of a food processor, add the chutney, grated cheddar cheese, sour cream and cream cheese. Sprinkle with salt and pepper to taste. Process until well combined.

2. Mix together the butter, curry powder and lemon juice in a separate bowl. Beat until fluffy.

3. Spread all of the bread slices with the curry butter. Cover half the slices with the cheddar cheese and chutney mixture. Press the other slices of bread on top. Trim off the crusts. Cut each sandwich into 4 triangles or squares. Place coriander onto a plate. Spread edges of sandwiches with mayonnaise. Roll edges in coriander. Arrange onto a platter.

Smoked Salmon Tea Sandwiches

INGREDIENTS

10 oz. smoked salmon
6 oz. cream cheese
1 teaspoon fresh lemon juice
4 tablespoons unsalted butter, softened
1 teaspoon chopped fresh tarragon or dill
1 small shallot, chopped finely
salt and freshly ground black pepper
8 slices whole wheat sandwich bread
Fresh sprigs of parsley &
lemon slices for garnish

INSTRUCTIONS

1. In a small bowl combine the butter with the shallots and herbs. Mix well. Spread the bread slices with the herb butter.

2. Spread cream cheese onto half of the bread slices.

3. Lay the slices of smoked salmon on top. Sprinkle over the lemon juice and add a generous grinding of fresh ground black pepper.

4. Press the remaining bread slices on top to form 4 sandwiches.

5. Trim off the crusts. Cut each sandwich into 4 triangles.

6. Place sandwiches onto a serving platter. Garnish platter with sprigs of parsley and thinly cut slices of lemon.

Rosemary Chicken Salad Tea Sandwiches

INGREDIENTS

3 cups cooked boneless chicken, cut into small cubes
1/2 cup mayonnaise
1/3 cup chopped green onion
1 teaspoon minced fresh rosemary
1/2 cup chopped smoked almonds
salt and pepper
8 slices of whole wheat sandwich bread
4 tablespoons unsalted butter, softened
1 teaspoon whole-grain Dijon style mustard
fresh parsley sprigs for garnish

INSTRUCTIONS

1. In a bowl mix together, the cooked diced chicken, mayonnaise, green onion and rosemary. Add the chopped nuts. Season to taste with salt and freshly ground black pepper.

2. In a separate small bowl combine the butter with the mustard. Mix well. Spread the bread slices with the mustard butter.

3. Cover half of the bread slices with the chicken salad. Press the other slices of bread on top.

4. Trim off the crusts. Cut each sandwich into 4 triangles. Place the sandwiches onto a serving platter. Decorate each of the triangles with a small sprig of parsley.

Cream Cheese & Date Tea Sandwiches

INGREDIENTS

3 oz. dried pitted dates, chopped
6 oz. cream cheese, softened
8 slices of cinnamon and raisin sandwich bread
4 tablespoons unsalted butter, softened
fresh sprigs of mint

INSTRUCTIONS

1. Chop the dates fine. In a small bowl combine the dates and cream cheese. Mix well until combined.

2 Spread bread slices with the butter. Spread half of the bread slices with the cream cheese mixture. Press the other slices of bread on top to form 4 sandwiches.

3. Trim off the crusts. Cut each sandwich into 3 fingers. (make 2 parallel cuts to form 3 fingers) Place sandwiches onto a serving platter. Garnish each sandwich with a small sprig of mint. The tea sandwiches may be made up to 2 hours ahead, if they are covered tightly and refrigerated.

Curried Egg Salad Tea Sandwiches

INGREDIENTS

4 hard boiled eggs
1/4 cup mayonnaise
1/2 teaspoon curry powder
salt and pepper
1/2 teaspoon Dijon style mustard
4 slices of whole wheat sandwich bread
4 slices of white sandwich bread
4 tablespoons unsalted butter, softened
sprigs of watercress or alfalfa sprouts

INSTRUCTIONS

1. Peel and finely chop the hard boiled eggs.

2. In a small bowl combine the eggs, mayonnaise, curry powder and mustard. Season to taste with salt and fresh ground black pepper.

3. Spread the bread slices with butter. Divide the egg salad among the white bread slices. Spread evenly. Press the whole wheat bread slices on top to form 4 sandwiches.

4. Trim off the crusts. Cut each sandwich into 3 fingers. Place sandwiches onto a serving platter. Garnish each sandwich with a small sprig of watercress or put a little dab of mayonnaise and place a few sprouts on top of each finger.

Stilton, Walnut & Pear Tea Sandwiches

INGREDIENTS

6 oz. English Stilton cheese
1 ripe pear
2/3 cup walnuts, toasted
8 slices of whole wheat sandwich bread
4 tablespoons unsalted butter, softened
1 teaspoon chopped fresh tarragon or chervil
1 small shallot, chopped finely
salt and pepper
sprigs of fresh parsley

INSTRUCTIONS

1. Core the pear and slice thinly.

2. Toast the nuts in the oven, and finely chop.

3. Crumble the stilton, and place in a bowl. Add the chopped nuts, and mix to combine. The mixture will be very crumbly.

4. In a separate small bowl combine the butter with the shallots and herbs. Mix well. Spread the bread slices with the herb butter.

5. Divide the cheese-nut mixture among half of the bread slices. Spread evenly. Lay the sliced pears on top. Press the remaining bread slices on top to form 4 sandwiches.

6. Trim off the crusts. Cut each sandwich into 4 triangles. Place sandwiches onto a serving platter. Garnish platter with sprigs of parsley

Minted Radish Tea Sandwiches

INGREDIENTS

8 radishes, washed and trimmed
1/3 cup mint leaves, washed and finely chopped
1/3 cup mayonnaise
1 tablespoon sour cream
1 teaspoon Dijon style mustard
1 teaspoon grated lemon zest
1/2 teaspoon fresh lemon juice
salt and pepper
8 slices white sandwich bread
4 tablespoons unsalted butter, softened
sprigs of watercress

INSTRUCTIONS

1. Slice the radishes very thinly, almost paper thin.

2. Mix together the mint, mayonnaise, sour cream, mustard, lemon juice and lemon zest. Sprinkle with salt and pepper to taste.

3. Spread the bread slices with the butter.

4. Spread the lemon mayonnaise mixture among half of the bread slices. Lay the slices of radishes on top. Press the remaining bread slices on top to form 4 sandwiches.

5. Trim off the crusts. Cut each sandwich into 4 squares. Place sandwiches onto a serving platter. Garnish serving platter with sprigs of watercress.

Smoked Turkey & Arugula Tea Sandwiches

INGREDIENTS

3 large bunches of Arugula
1 green onion, chopped
1/3 cup mayonnaise
1/2 teaspoon grated lemon zest
1 tablespoon chopped fresh parsley
1 tablespoon chopped fresh thyme
3/4 lb. smoked turkey, sliced thinly
salt and pepper
8 slices white sandwich bread
4 tablespoons unsalted butter, softened
Fresh sprigs of flat leaf parsley for garnish

INSTRUCTIONS

1. Wash and chop the arugula.

2. In a medium bowl, mix together, the chopped green onion, chopped arugula mayonnaise, lemon zest, parsley, and thyme. Season with salt and pepper to taste.

3. Spread bread slices with the butter. Spread half of the bread slices with the mayonnaise mixture. Top these slices with the smoked turkey. Press the remaining slices of bread on top to form 4 sandwiches.

4. Trim off the crusts. Cut each sandwich into 4 triangles. Arrange sandwiches onto a serving platter. Garnish the sandwiches with sprigs of the flat leaf parsley

Cucumber & Mint Tea Sandwiches

INGREDIENTS

1/4 cup chopped fresh mint leaves (preferably spearmint)
6 oz. cream cheese, softened
8 slices of white sandwich bread
2/3 of a medium seedless cucumber, peeled and sliced thinly
4 tablespoons unsalted butter, softened
salt and pepper

INSTRUCTIONS

1. Rinse and dry mint and chop very fine.

2. In a small bowl combine the mint and cream cheese and mix until well combined.

3. Sprinkle salt and pepper over the cucumber slices. Reserve 16 of the cucumber slices for decoration.

4. Spread bread slices with the butter. Spread half of the bread slices with the mint-cream cheese mixture. Cover with slices of the cucumber. Press the other slices of bread on top to form 4 sandwiches.

5. Trim off the crusts. Cut each sandwich into 4 squares. (make 2 cuts in a crosswise fashion to form 4 quarters). Place sandwiches onto a serving platter. Decorate with the reserved cucumber slices. Garnish the platter with a few sprigs of mint.

Asparagus Gorgonzola Pinwheels

INGREDIENTS

8 asparagus, ends trimmed
6 oz. cream cheese
4 oz. gorgonzola cheese, crumbled
2 teaspoons chopped fresh marjoram or thyme
1 tablespoon chopped fresh parsley
salt and fresh ground black pepper
8 slices white sandwich bread
3 tablespoons butter, melted

INSTRUCTIONS

1. Blanch asparagus in boiling water for 3 minutes. Drain and rinse under cold water.

2. In a small bowl combine the cream cheese, gorgonzola, herbs, and chopped parsley. Mix well. Sprinkle with salt and pepper.

3. Using a rolling pin, flatten the bread slices. Divide and spread the cheese mixture evenly among the bread slices.

4. Trim off the crusts. Place a blanched asparagus on top of each bread slice. Roll each slice of bread, pressing together firmly to hold. Wrap each roll in plastic wrap and refrigerate for 1-2 hours.

5. Slice each roll into thirds. Place pinwheels onto a baking sheet. Brush the tops and sides with melted butter. Place under broiler in oven for approximately 2 1/2 minutes or until lightly browned.
Serve immediately.

Olive Pinwheels

INGREDIENTS

4 tablespoons unsalted butter, softened
1 teaspoon chopped fresh rosemary or thyme
1 small shallot, chopped finely
1/2 cup pimento stuffed green olives, finely chopped
1 teaspoon fresh lemon juice
salt and freshly ground black pepper
6 oz. cream cheese
8 slices whole wheat sandwich bread
sprigs of watercress

INSTRUCTIONS

1. In a small bowl combine the butter with the shallots and herbs. Mix well. Spread the bread slices with the herb butter.

2. Combine the chopped olives with the lemon juice, salt and freshly ground pepper. Mix well.

3. Using a rolling pin, flatten the bread slices. Spread the cream cheese onto the bread slices. Trim off the crusts.

4. Sprinkle the olives evenly among the bread slices. Roll each slice of bread, pressing together firmly to hold. Wrap each roll in plastic wrap and refrigerate for 1-2 hours.

5. When ready to serve, unwrap each roll, and slice into 4 pinwheels. Place pinwheels onto a serving platter, and decorate with sprigs of watercress.

Smoked Salmon Pinwheels

INGREDIENTS

8 oz. smoked salmon
6 oz. cream cheese, softened
2 tablespoons chopped fresh parsley
2 teaspoons fresh lemon juice
2 tablespoons cream
1 teaspoon chopped dill
salt and freshly ground black pepper
4 tablespoons unsalted butter, softened
8 slices white sandwich bread
lemon slices for garnish

INSTRUCTIONS

1. In a food processor, combine the smoked salmon, cream cheese, parsley, lemon juice, cream, dill, salt and pepper. Process until mixture becomes a smooth spreading consistency.

2. Spread the slices of bread with butter. Then spread the salmon-cream cheese mixture evenly on the bread slices.

3. Trim off the crusts. Roll each slice of bread, pressing together firmly to hold. Wrap each roll in plastic wrap and refrigerate for 2-3 hours.

4. When ready to serve, unwrap each roll, and slice into 4 pinwheels. Place pinwheels onto a platter, and garnish with lemon slices.

Chicken in Puff Pastry

INGREDIENTS

1 lb. package of prepared frozen puff pastry shells
1 egg, beaten
3 tablespoons butter
3 tablespoons flour
12 oz. fresh or canned chicken broth
salt and pepper
dash of cayenne pepper
8 oz. mushrooms, sliced thinly
1 lb. chicken breast, cut into small pieces
2 tablespoons olive oil
2 teaspoons chopped fresh rosemary or thyme

INSTRUCTIONS

1. Place the thawed individual pastry shells onto a greased baking sheet. Brush with beaten egg. Bake 20-25 min. in a preheated oven at 425°F.

2. When pastry has cooled, remove the center lid with a fork. Scoop out a little of the soft inner pastry, to make room for the filling.

3. Heat the olive oil in a saute pan over medium high heat. Add the mushrooms and cook for 2 minutes stirring constantly. Add the chicken pieces and continue to cook until browned. Sprinkle with the herbs, salt and pepper. Transfer mixture to a medium bowl.

4. In the same saute pan, add the butter. When it has melted, add the flour, stirring constantly, for a minute. Gradually whisk in the chicken broth and continue to cook until the sauce has thickened, stirring constantly. Add the dash of cayenne. Remove pan from heat and allow sauce to cool.

5. Pour the sauce over the cooked chicken-mushroom mixture. Stir well to combine. Spoon the mixture into the pastry shells and replace lids. Decorate each shell with a sprig of fresh herb or parsley.

Savory Salmon in Filo

INGREDIENTS

8 sheets of frozen prepared Filo dough
12 oz. salmon filet, boneless, skinless
4 tablespoons butter, melted
6 oz. feta cheese, crumbled
2 cloves garlic, minced
1/2 teaspoon paprika
salt and pepper
2 tablespoon mayonnaise
10 Kalmata olives, pitted and chopped
1 tablespoons olive oil
2 teaspoons Dijon style mustard
1 teaspoon fresh lemon juice

INSTRUCTIONS

1. Cut salmon filet into 8 even pieces. Place in a bowl, and add; garlic, paprika, salt and pepper to taste, mayonnaise, chopped olives, olive oil, mustard and lemon juice. Turn to coat the salmon with the mixture.

2. Carefully take one sheet of the thawed filo dough and place it onto the work surface, while keeping the rest of the filo dough covered with a slightly damp tea towel. Brush the sheet of filo with melted butter. Top with the next sheet of filo, & brush again with butter. Repeat this with 2 more sheets of filo., so that you have 4 layers.

3. Cut the layered filo into 4 strips, across the width. Place a piece of salmon on one corner. Top with some of the feta. Fold the corner over and over again as if folding a flag, to form a neat triangle package. Brush with butter. Repeat this process using the other 3 strips of filo.

4. Repeat steps #2 through # 3 one more time, so that there will be 8 salmon packages total. Bake in preheated oven at 400°F for 20 min.

Scones, Muffins
&
Tea Breads

Currant Scones

INGREDIENTS

2 cups unbleached flour
3 tablespoons sugar
1 tablespoon baking powder
1/2 teaspoon salt
1/2 teaspoon nutmeg
1/2 cup butter, unsalted, cut into pieces
1/3 cup milk
1 large egg, beaten
2/3 cup currants

INSTRUCTIONS

1. Preheat oven to 450°F. Into the bowl of a food processor, add the flour, sugar, baking powder, nutmeg and salt. Pulse on and off to combine. Add the butter, and process until mixture is coarse.

2. Add the milk and 1/2 of the beaten egg to the food processor bowl, and continue to pulse *just* until the dough forms large pieces.

3. Turn out the dough onto a lightly floured bread board. Knead the currants into the dough.

4. Pat the dough out with your hands to form a circle 1/2" thick. Using a 2 1/2" round biscuit cutter, dipped in flour, cut the dough into 12 rounds.

5. Place the scones onto a greased baking sheet. Refrigerate for 20 minutes, or until ready to use. Brush tops with the remaining half of the beaten egg. Bake for 15 minutes. Cool. Serve scones with jam and clotted cream.

Lemon Cream Scones

INGREDIENTS

2 cups unbleached flour

1/3 cup sugar

1 tablespoon baking powder

1/4 teaspoon salt

1/2 cup golden raisins

1 teaspoon lemon peel, grated fine

1 cup whipping cream

3 tablespoons water

1 egg, beaten

INSTRUCTIONS

1. Preheat oven to 375°F. In a large mixing bowl, add the flour, sugar, baking powder and salt. Stir in the raisins and lemon zest.

2. Slowly stir in the cream to the bowl and the 3 tablespoons water. Using a fork, continue to stir *just* until the dough is formed.

3. Turn out the dough onto a lightly floured bread board and knead the dough for a minute.

4. Place the dough onto a greased baking sheet. Lightly press the dough with your hands to form an 8 inch circle.

5. With a knife, that has been dipped in flour, cut almost all the way through the dough into 12 wedges as in a pie. Brush tops with the beaten egg. Bake for 25-30 minutes.

Cinnamon Pecan Cream Scones

INGREDIENTS

1 cup all-purpose flour
3 tablespoons sugar
1 1/2 teaspoons baking powder
1/4 teaspoon baking soda
1/2 teaspoon cinnamon
1/4 teaspoon salt
3 tablespoons butter, unsalted, cut into pieces
1/4 cup heavy cream
1 large egg yolk
1/2 teaspoon vanilla
1/3 cup pecans, chopped
1/3 cup dried currants

INSTRUCTIONS

1. Preheat oven to 400°F. Into the bowl of a food processor, add the flour, sugar, baking powder, baking soda, cinnamon and salt. Pulse on and off to combine. Add the butter bits, and process for approx. 10 seconds or until the mixture is like coarse meal.

2. Add cream, egg yolk, and vanilla. Process for a few more seconds, just until the dough forms.

3. Turn out the dough onto a floured bread board. Knead the pecans and currants into the dough.

4. Pat the dough out with your hands to form a circle 3/4"thick. Cut the circle into 6 wedges. Transfer each wedge onto a greased baking sheet. Brush tops with a beaten egg. Sprinkle with a little sugar. Bake for 15 minutes or until they are golden.

Cardamom Nut Scones

INGREDIENTS

2 1/4 cups flour
3 tablespoons brown sugar
1 tablespoon baking powder
1/2 teaspoon baking soda
2 teaspoons ground cardamom
1/4 teaspoon cinnamon
1/4 teaspoon freshly grated nutmeg
2 teaspoons grated lemon zest
1/2 teaspoon salt
6 tablespoons unsalted butter, cut into pieces
1/2 cup milk
1 egg, large
1 teaspoon vanilla
1/3 cup walnuts, toasted

INSTRUCTIONS

1. Preheat oven to 400°F. Into the bowl of a food processor, add the flour, brown sugar, baking powder, baking soda, cardamom, cinnamon, nutmeg, lemon zest, and salt. Pulse on and off to combine. Add the butter bits, and process for approx. 10 seconds or until the mixture is like coarse meal. Add the milk, egg, and vanilla. Process for a few more seconds, just until the dough forms.

2. Turn out the dough onto a floured bread board. Knead the walnuts into the dough. Pat the dough out with your hands to form a circle 3/4" thick. Using a 2 1/2" round biscuit cutter, dipped in flour, cut the dough into 12 rounds. Place the scones onto a greased baking sheet. Brush tops with a beaten egg. Bake 17 minutes, until golden.

Cheddar Cornmeal Scones

INGREDIENTS

3/4 cup all-purpose flour
1/2 cup yellow cornmeal
2 teaspoons sugar
1 1/4 teaspoons baking powder
1/2 teaspoon salt
a dash of cayenne
3 tablespoons unsalted butter, cut into pieces
3/4 cup grated sharp Cheddar Cheese
1 large egg yolk
1/3 cup milk

INSTRUCTIONS

1. Preheat oven to 425°F. Into the bowl of a food processor, add the flour, cornmeal, sugar, baking powder, cayenne, and salt. Pulse on and off to combine. Add the butter bits, and process for approx. 10 seconds or until the mixture is like coarse meal. Add the grated cheese, milk, and egg yolk. Process for a few more seconds, *just* until the dough forms.

2. Turn out the dough onto a floured bread board. Knead the dough about 10 times. Pat the dough out with your hands to form an 8 inch circle. Using a knife, dipped in flour, cut the dough into 6 wedges.

3. Place the wedges onto a greased baking sheet. Brush tops with a beaten egg. Sprinkle with a little additional grated cheddar cheese. Bake for 17 minutes, or until golden.

Lemon Cranberry Scones

INGREDIENTS

1 1/4 cups fresh cranberries, chopped coarsely
2 1/2 cups all-purpose flour
1/2 cup sugar
1 tablespoon baking powder
1/2 teaspoon salt
2 tablespoons grated lemon zest
6 tablespoons unsalted butter, cut into pieces
1 large egg, beaten
1 large egg yolk, for brushing
1 cup heavy cream

INSTRUCTIONS

1. Preheat oven to 400°F. Using a food processor, chop the cranberries, coarsely. Transfer cranberries to a large bowl. Into the food processor, add the flour, sugar, baking powder, salt, grated lemon zest, and the butter bits. Pulse on and off to combine. until the mixture is like coarse meal. Pour out this flour mixture into the bowl with the cranberries. Stir to combine.

2. Add the beaten egg and cream to the bowl. Stir just until the dough forms.

3. Turn out the dough onto a floured bread board. Pat the dough out with your hands to form an 8 inch circle. Using a 2" round biscuit cutter, dipped in flour, cut the dough into 12- 16 rounds. Place the scones onto a greased baking sheet. Brush tops of scones with a beaten egg yolk and sprinkle with a little extra granulated sugar. Bake 18 minutes, or until golden.

Nut & Raisin Sticky Scones

INGREDIENTS

4 cups unbleached flour
1/3 cup brown sugar
1 tablespoon baking powder
1/4 teaspoon baking soda
1 egg
4 tablespoons butter, cut into pieces
1 1/2 cup buttermilk
1/2 cup raisins
1 cup pecans, chopped
4 tablespoons butter, melted
3/4 cup brown sugar
1 tablespoon honey
1 tablespoon molasses

INSTRUCTIONS

1. Preheat oven to 375°F. In a large mixing bowl, add the flour, 1/3 cup brown sugar, baking powder and baking soda. Stir. Add the egg and butter pats and beat at low speed with an electric mixer for a minute.

2. Slowly add the buttermilk to the bowl, and continue to beat *just* until the dough is formed. Do not over beat.

3. Turn out the dough onto a floured bread board and lightly press out the dough to form a rectangle, approx. 1" thick. Sprinkle the dough with the raisins and nuts. Roll up the dough from the long side, to form a log. Cut into 8-10 slices.

4. In a small bowl, mix together; the melted butter, 3/4 cup brown sugar, honey and molasses. Pour this mixture into a buttered 9 x 13 baking pan. Place the sliced rolls into the baking dish. Bake for 28 minutes.

Lemon Curd

INGREDIENTS

4 eggs
1 1/4 cups sugar
4 lemons
12 tablespoons unsalted butter

INSTRUCTIONS

1. Juice the 4 lemons and reserve the juice. Grate the rind of 2 of the lemons.

2. Using an electric mixer, beat together sugar and eggs until light and fluffy. Beat in the lemon juice.

3. Pour the lemon mixture into a saucepan and cook over low heat while stirring constantly. Gradually add the butter, 1 tablespoon at a time. Keep stirring until all of the butter is melted and combined with the egg mixture. Raise the heat to medium and continue to cook and stir the mixture until it is thickened. Stir in the lemon zest.

4. Pour mixture into clean dry jars and cover tightly. Store in the refrigerator. This lemon curd is delicious when served with scones. It may also be used as a filling for tarts.

Clotted Cream

INGREDIENTS

1 cup heavy whipping cream
1/3 cup sour cream
1 tablespoon powdered sugar

INSTRUCTIONS

1. Bring the whipping cream and sour cream to room temperature. Pour the whipping cream into a bowl and beat it with an electric mixer until soft peaks form.

2. Add the sour cream and powdered sugar to the bowl. Beat until the mixture is very thick.

3. Place in refrigerator until ready to serve. Put into individual small serving dishes. This "mock" clotted cream is delicious served with scones.

Fruit Butters

INGREDIENTS

2 sticks butter (1/2 lb.), room temperature
1/2 cup preserves; strawberry, raspberry or orange marmalade

INSTRUCTIONS

Place butter and preserves in a bowl. Using an electric mixer, beat until light and fluffy. Put mixture into individual serving dishes and serve with tea breads or scones.

Almond Lemon Tea Bread

INGREDIENTS

2 large lemons
3 cups flour
2 teaspoons baking powder
1/4 teaspoon salt
1 1/2 sticks unsalted butter, softened
1 teaspoon almond extract
1 1/2 cups sugar
4 large eggs
1 cup milk
1 tablepoon poppy seeds
1/2 cup confectioners sugar, for glaze

INSTRUCTIONS

1. Preheat oven to 325°F. Butter two 9- x 5 inch loaf pans.

2. Grate the zest of the lemons and squeeze out the lemon juice, and reserve. In a large separate bowl beat together with an electric mixer, the butter, almond extract, sugar, and lemon zest. Beat until light and fluffy. Add in eggs and beat well. Beat in the milk. On low speed add the flour, baking powder, and salt. Beat *just* until batter is combined. Do not over beat Stir in poppy seeds and 2 tablespoons of the lemon juice

3 Pour batter into the 2 loaf pans. Bake for 50-55 minutes.

4. To make the glaze; stir together, in a small bowl, the remaining lemon juice and the confectioners sugar. After loaves have cooled for 10 minutes, pierce tops all over with a toothpick. Brush the lemon glaze over the loaves. Allow the loaves to absorb all of the glaze. Cool completely before serving. Slice tea bread and arrange onto a serving platter.

Banana Nut Tea Bread

INGREDIENTS

3 bananas
2 eggs
1/2 cup water
1/2 cup vegetable oil
3/4 cup sugar
2 cups flour
1 teaspoon baking soda
1/2 teaspoon salt
1 teaspoon cinnamon
1/2 teaspoon nutmeg
1/2 cup walnuts, toasted

INSTRUCTIONS

1. Preheat oven to 350°F. Butter a 9 x 5 inch loaf pan.

2. Peel and mash bananas in a large mixing bowl. Add in the eggs, water, oil and sugar. Using an electric mixer, beat until light and fluffy

3. Stir in the flour, baking soda, salt, cinnamon and nutmeg. Stir *just* until batter is combined. Do not over beat. Chop the toasted walnuts, and fold into the banana tea bread batter.

4. Pour batter into the the prepared loaf pan. Bake for 45 minutes. or until a skewer inserted into the center comes out. Cool completely before serving. Slice tea bread and arrange onto a serving platter.

Wendy's Cranberry Tea Bread

INGREDIENTS

1 cup fresh cranberries, coarsley chopped
1/2 cup walnuts, chopped
grated zest of 1 orange
2 cups flour
1 cup sugar
1 1/2 teaspoons baking powder
1/2 teaspoon baking soda
1 teaspoon salt
2 tablespoons butter
1 egg, beaten
3/4 cup fresh squeezed orange juice

INSTRUCTIONS

1. Preheat oven to 350°F. Butter and flour a 9 x 5 inch loaf pan.

2. Chop cranberries and walnuts. Grate orange peel. Set aside. Squeeze the orange and reserve juice.

3. In a large bowl, mix together: flour, sugar, baking powder, baking soda, and salt. Cut in the butter with a pastry blender. Stir in egg, orange juice, and orange zest. Mix just until moistened. Do not overbeat. Fold in the chopped cranberries and nuts. Spoon into the prepared pan.

4. Bake 1 hour or until a skewer inserted into the center comes out clean. Cool 20 minutes before slicing and serving.

Blueberry Muffins

INGREDIENTS

1 cup blueberries
1/2 cup sugar
2cups flour
1 teaspoon cinnamon
1 tablespoon baking powder
2 eggs
1 cup milk
5 tablespoons butter, melted
3 tablespoons brown sugar

INSTRUCTIONS

1. Preheat oven to 350°F. Place 12 paper muffin cup liners into muffin tins. Wash blueberries and allow to drain in a strainer.

2. In a large mixing bowl, mix together: sugar, flour, cinnamon and baking powder.

3. Add to the bowl: eggs, milk, melted butter, and blueberries. Stir *just* until the batter is combined. Do not overbeat.

4 Spoon batter into the muffin cups. Sprinkle tops with the brown sugar. Bake for 25 minutes

Pecan Muffins

INGREDIENTS

1/2 cup pecans, toasted and chopped
1/2 cup sugar
2 cups flour
1 tablespoon baking powder
1/2 teaspoon salt
1 egg
1 cup milk
5 tablespoons butter, melted
For Topping:
1 teaspoon cinnamon
3 tablespoons sugar
1/4 cup chopped pecans

INSTRUCTIONS

1. Preheat oven to 375°F. Place 12 paper muffin cup liners into muffin tins. Toast and chop pecans.

2. In a large mixing bowl, mix together: sugar, flour, baking powder, and salt..

3. Add to the bowl: egg, milk, and melted butter. Stir *just* until the batter is moistened. Fold in the 1/2 cup toasted and chopped pecans.

4. For the topping, mix together: cinnamon, sugar and 1/4 cup chopped pecans.

5. Spoon batter into the muffin cups. Sprinkle tops of muffins with the sugar and nut mixture. Bake for 20 minutes.

Zucchini Bread

INGREDIENTS

2 cups grated raw zucchini
1 1/4 cup sugar
3/4 cup vegetable oil
3 eggs
1 teaspoon vanilla extract
2 1/2 cups flour
2 teaspoons baking powder
1 teaspoon baking soda
1/2 teaspoon salt
1 teaspoon cinnamon
1/2 teaspoon cloves
1 cup walnuts, toasted and chopped

INSTRUCTIONS

1. Preheat oven to 350°F. Butter a 9x5 inch loaf pan. Grate the zucchini. It is not necessary to peel it. Toast and chop the walnuts.

2. In a large mixing bowl, beat together: sugar, oil, eggs, and vanilla. Beat until light. Stir in the grated zucchini.

3. Add to the bowl: flour, baking powder, baking soda, salt, cinnamon, and cloves. Stir *just* until the batter is moistened. Fold in the chopped nuts.

4. Pour batter into the prepared loaf pan. Bake for 1 hour and 10 minutes or until a skewer inserted into the center comes out clean. Cool bread before slicing. Arrange slices onto a serving platter.

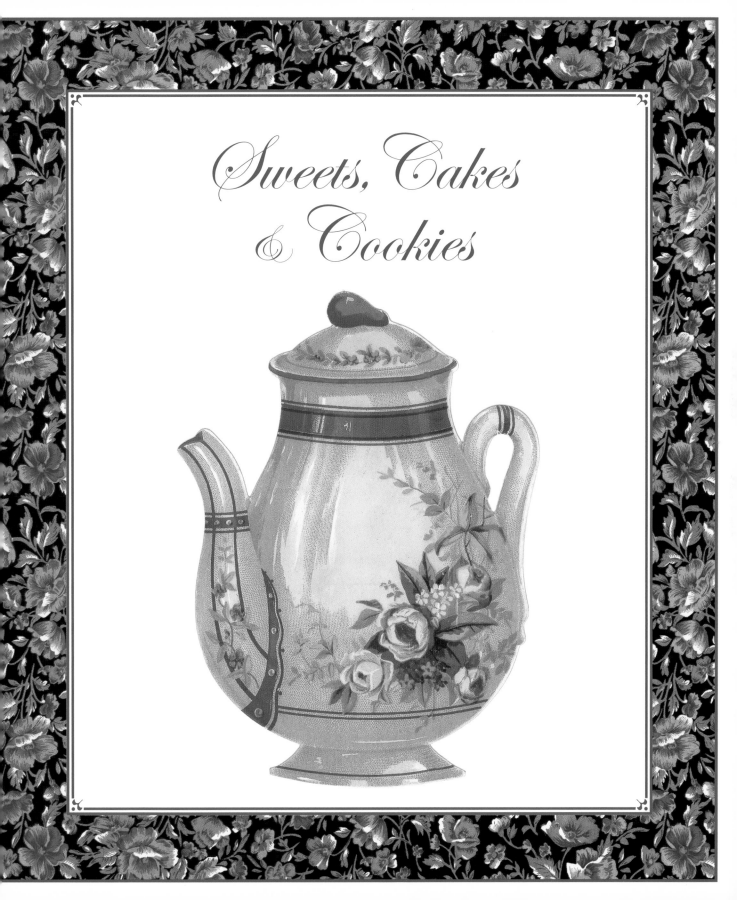

Sweets, Cakes
& Cookies

Blueberry Pear Tarts

INGREDIENTS

PASTRY

1 2/3 cups flour
1/3 cup sugar
1/4 teaspoon salt
1 1/4 sticks butter
2 small egg yolks
1 teaspoon vanilla extract
2 teaspoons ice cold water

PASTRY CREAM

2 cups milk
3 whole eggs
1/2 cup sugar
6 tablespoons flour
1 teaspoon vanilla extract

TOPPING

1/2 cup blueberries
1/2 cup thinly sliced poached pears
2 tablespoons apricot preserves

INSTRUCTIONS

1. Butter 12 4" miniature pie tart tins.

2. Pastry: Mix the flour, sugar, and salt in a mixing bowl. Cut in the cold butter using your fingertips or a pastry blender until the mixture resembles coarse meal. Whisk together the 2 egg yolks, vanilla and water. Add this to the flour mixture and blend with a fork. Shape the dough into a ball and wrap in plastic and refrigerate for 1-2 hours. Preheat oven to 375°. Roll out pastry 1/4" thick. Cut out rounds of pastry and press neatly into the buttered tins. Bake for 10-12 min. or until golden brown. Cool

3. Pastry Cream: Put milk in saucepan, and let it come to a boil. Then cool slightly. Whisk together in a bowl; the 3 eggs and sugar. Add the flour, vanilla and a little of the warm milk. Blend. Add this egg mixture to the pan of warm milk. Over medium heat, stirring constantly, cook until custard comes to a boil and is smooth and thick. Let mixture cool completely. Fill the baked tarts shells with the pastry cream. Top each tart with the slices of pear and blueberries. Warm the apricot preserves and brush over the fruit. Let set. Insert a skewer down the sides of the tin, and gently remove pastry to a plate.

Strawberry Tarts

INGREDIENTS

PASTRY
1 2/3 cups flour
1/3 cup sugar
1/4 teaspoon salt
1 1/4 sticks butter
2 small egg yolks
1 teaspoon vanilla extract
2 teaspoons ice cold water

PASTRY CREAM
2 cups milk
3 whole eggs
1/2 cup sugar
6 tablespoons flour
1 teaspoon vanilla extract

TOPPING
1 lb. strawberries, hulled and sliced
5 tablespoons red current jelly

INSTRUCTIONS

1. Preheat oven to 350°F. Butter 12 4" miniature pie tart tins.

2. Pastry: Mix the flour, sugar, and salt in a mixing bowl. Cut in the cold butter using your fingertips or a pastry blender until the mixture resembles coarse meal. Whisk together the 2 egg yolks, vanilla and water. Add this to the flour mixture and blend with a fork. Shape the dough into a ball and wrap in plastic and refrigerate for 1-2 hours. Roll out pastry on a floured board 1/4" thick. Cut out rounds of pastry and press neatly into the buttered tins. Bake for 10 min. or until golden brown. Cool

3. Pastry Cream: Put milk in saucepan, and let it come to a boil. Then cool slightly. Whisk together in a bowl; the 3 eggs and sugar. Add the flour, vanilla and a little of the warm milk. Blend. Add this egg mixture to the pan of warm milk. Over medium heat, stirring constantly, cook until custard comes to a boil and is smooth and thick. Let mixture cool completely. Fill the baked tarts shells halfway with the pastry cream. Arrange the sliced strawberries neatly over the custard. Warm the current jelly and brush the glaze all over the fruit to seal it. Let set a while before serving.

Pecan Squares

INGREDIENTS

CRUST

2 cups flour
3/4 cup confectioners' sugar
2 sticks butter (1/2 lb.)

TOPPING

1/2 cup honey
1/2 cup brown sugar
1/4 cup heavy cream
1 stick butter, melted
1/2 teaspoon maple extract
3 1/4 cups pecans, chopped

INSTRUCTIONS

1. Preheat oven to 350°F. Butter a 13x9 inch baking pan.

2. Crust: In a mixing bowl, stir together the flour and confectioners' sugar. Using a pastry blender or your fingertips, cut in the butter until the mixture is like coarse meal. Pour this mixture into the buttered baking pan. Press mixture evenly onto the bottom of the baking pan to form the crust. Bake 20 minutes. Remove from oven.

3. Topping: Mix together: the honey, brown sugar, cream, melted butter, and maple extract. Fold in the chopped pecans. Pour this mixture over the baked crust. Bake another 25 minutes. Cool pan for 1/2 hour and cut into squares.

Lemon Squares

INGREDIENTS

CRUST
2 sticks butter (1/2 lb.)
1/2 cup confectioners' sugar
2 cups flour

TOPPING
4 eggs
1 3/4 cup granulated sugar
1 1/4 teaspoon baking powder
1/4 cup lemon juice
grated rind of 2 lemons
1/4 cup flour

INSTRUCTIONS

1. Preheat oven to 350°F. Butter a 13x9 inch baking pan.

2. Crust: With an electric mixer at low speed, beat together the butter, confectioners' sugar, and flour. Beat until the mixture is like coarse meal. Pour this mixture into the buttered baking pan. Press mixture evenly onto the bottom of the baking pan to form the crust. Bake 20 minutes. Remove from oven.

3. Topping: Beat together: the eggs, sugar, baking powder, lemon juice, lemon rind and the 1/4 cup flour. Beat until light and fluffy. Pour this mixture over the baked crust. Bake another 25 minutes. Cool pan for 1/2 hour and cut into squares.

Chocolate Pecan Toffee Bars

INGREDIENTS

2 sticks butter (1/2 lb.)
3/4 cup light brown sugar
1/4 cup granulated sugar
1 egg yolk
2 cups flour
1 teaspoon vanilla extract
1 large pkg. chocolate chips (12 oz.)
1 cup pecans, toasted and chopped

INSTRUCTIONS

1. Preheat oven to 350°F. Butter a 13 x 9 inch baking pan. Toast and chop the nuts and set aside.

2. With an electric mixer at low speed, cream together the butter, brown sugar and granulated sugar. Add the egg yolk and vanilla extract. Beat well. Stir in the flour.

3. Spread this mixture onto the buttered baking pan. Bake 25 minutes. Remove from oven.

4. Sprinkle top with the chocolate chips. Return pan to the oven for 3 minutes. Using a knife, spread the melted chocolate evenly across the surface of the pan. Sprinkle with the chopped nuts. Cool completely and cut into squares.

White Chip Walnut Bars

INGREDIENTS

3/4 cup vegetable shortening
1 1/2 cup light brown sugar
2 large eggs
2 teaspoons vanilla extract
1 teaspoon cinnamon
2 1/2 cups flour
1 1/2 teaspoon baking powder
1/2 teaspoon salt
2 cups white chocolate chips (12 oz. pkg.)
1 cup walnuts toasted and chopped

INSTRUCTIONS

1. Preheat oven to 350°F. Butter a 13 x 9 inch baking pan. Toast and chop the walnuts and set aside.

2. With an electric mixer at low speed, cream together the shortening and brown sugar. Add the eggs, vanilla extract, and cinnamon. Beat well. Stir in the flour, baking powder, salt. Mix *just* until combined. Fold in the chips and nuts.

3. Spread the batter into the buttered baking pan. Bake 28-30 minutes. Allow to cool completely before serving. Cut into squares.

Almond Butter Bars

INGREDIENTS

1 cup almond butter
6 tablespoons butter, softened
2/3 cup light brown sugar, packed
1/2 cup granulated sugar
3 eggs
1 teaspoons vanilla extract
1 cup flour
2 cups chocolate chips (12 oz. pkg.)

INSTRUCTIONS

1. Preheat oven to 350°F. Butter a 13 x 9 inch baking pan.

2. Beat together, with an electric mixer at low speed, the almond butter, brown sugar and granulated sugar. Beat in the eggs, and vanilla extract. Beat until creamy. Stir in the flour. Mix *just* until combined. Fold in 3/4 cup of the chocolate chips., reserving the rest for the frosting.

3. Spread the batter into the buttered baking pan. Bake 20-25 minutes. Remove pan from the oven and sprinkle with the remaining chips. Let stand for a few minutes until the chips have melted. Using a knife, spread the chocolate evenly across the top of bars. Allow to cool completely before serving. Cut into fingers and arrange onto a serving tray.

Rugelach Pastries

INGREDIENTS

PASTRY
2 sticks butter (1/2 lb.)
8 ounces cream cheese
1/3 cup sugar
2 cups flour
1 tablespoon cold water

FILLING # 1
1/2 cup sugar
2 teaspoons cinnamon
1/2 cup raisins
1 cup walnuts, chopped fine
additional sugar for topping

FILLING # 2
1 cup strawberry or apricot
preserves
1 cup almonds, chopped fine
1/4 teaspoon almond extract
additional sugar for topping

INSTRUCTIONS

1. Pastry: In a large mixing bowl, add butter, cream cheese, and sugar. Beat with an electric mixer until well blended. Add the flour little by little and blend just until the dough is formed. Blend in the 1 tablespoon water. Shape the dough into a ball. Sprinkle the dough with a little flour and wrap in plastic and refrigerate for 2 hours.

2. Filling #1: in a bowl, mix together: 1/2 cup sugar, cinnamon, raisins and chopped walnuts. Filling #2: in a separate bowl, mix together: preserves, chopped almonds and almond extract.

3 Preheat oven to 350°F. Butter 2 cookie sheets. Divide the dough into 4 sections. Roll out one section at a time on a floured board to make a 10" circle. Sprinkle circle of pastry with 1/2 of filling #1. Using a knife or pastry wheel cut the circle like a pie into 12 wedges. Beginning at the wide edge, roll each wedge up toward the point, to form a crescent. Repeat process for the other 3 sections of pastry and remainder of both fillings. Place the rolled crescents onto the buttered cookie sheet. Sprinkle the top of each pastry with a little sugar. Bake 25 minutes.

REAL WEDGWOOD STONEWARE.

3042

3042

3042

3042

3043

3042

3042

3043

3043

3043

3044

3044

3044

3045

3045

3045

3045

3045

3044

3045

REAL WEDGWOOD STONEWARE.

Coconut Cake

INGREDIENTS

COCONUT CAKE
3/4 cup shortening
1 cup granulated sugar
3 eggs, separated
1 teaspoon vanilla extract
2 1/4 cups all-purpose flour
2 teaspoon baking powder
1/2 teaspoon salt

1 cup milk
2 cups shredded coconut, sweetened

COCONUT FROSTING
4 tablespoons butter, melted
1/4 cup cream
3 cups confectioners' sugar
1/2 cup shredded coconut, sweetened

INSTRUCTIONS

1. Preheat oven to 350°F. Butter and lightly flour two 9 "round cake pans.

2. With an electric mixer at low speed, cream together the shortening and sugar, until light. Add egg yolks and vanilla extract beating well. Add in the flour, baking powder, salt and milk. Beat until well blended. Stir in 1 cup of the shredded coconut.

3. In a separate bowl, beat egg whites until stiff peaks form, but not dry. Stir in 1/3 of the egg whites into the cake batter. Then gently fold in the remainder of the egg whites. Spoon batter into the prepared cake pans.

4. Bake 25 minutes or until a skewer inserted into the middle, comes out clean.. Let the cakes cool in the pan. Lightly toast the remaining 1 cup of coconut, and reserve this for decorating the frosted cake.

5 Frosting: Add melted butter and cream to a mixing bowl. Beat in confectioners' sugar, a little at a time, until frosting is thick and creamy. Beat in the 1 /2 cup shredded coconut. When the cakes are cool, invert the first layer onto a serving plate. Frost the top of this layer. Invert the second layer on top of the first layer. Frost the top and sides of the cake. Decorate cake on the top and sides using the reserved toasted coconut.

Chocolate Cherry Cakes

INGREDIENTS

1/3 cup maraschino cherries
2 tablespoons framboise or other raspberry liqueur
4 ounces semi sweet chocolate, chopped
4 tablespoons butter
1/2 cup sugar
1/2 teaspoon vanilla
2 large eggs
1/2 cup flour
1/4 teaspoon salt
1/2 cup confectioners' sugar for decorating cakes

INSTRUCTIONS

1. Preheat oven to 350°F. Butter a 6-cup muffin tin. Chop the maraschino cherries and pour the liqueur over the cherries, and reserve.

2. Melt chocolate and butter together in a double boiler, over lightly simmering water. Stir until smooth. Remove pan from heat and stir in the sugar and vanilla. Whisk in the eggs, beating well. Stir in the flour and salt. Mix *just* until combined. Fold in the cherries.

3. Spoon the batter into the prepared muffin tin.

4. Bake 20 minutes. Cool in pan for 15 minutes. Place a doily over the top of each cake and sift confectioners' sugar over the top. Carefully remove the doily. Arrange cakes onto a serving platter.

Rum Cake

INGREDIENTS

3 cups flour
1 1/2 teaspoon baking soda
1/2 teaspoon salt
12 oz. semisweet chocolate chips
1 cup vegetable shortening or butter
1 cup strong coffee
1/3 cup dark rum
2 1/4 cups sugar
3 eggs
2 teaspoons vanilla
confectioners' sugar for dusting
whipped cream
raspberries
cocoa powder for dusting

INSTRUCTIONS

1. Preheat oven to 300°F. Butter a bundt cake pan and dust with cocoa powder. Shake out excess.

2. Melt chocolate and shortening (or butter) together in a large metal mixing bowl set over lightly simmering water. Stir until smooth. Remove bowl from heat and stir in the coffee, rum, and sugar. Using an electric mixer, beat in the eggs and vanilla. Add the flour, baking soda and salt. Mix *just* until combined.

3. Spoon batter into the prepared bundt cake pan. Bake 1 hour and 30 min. or until skewer inserted comes out clean. Cool in pan. Invert cake onto serving plate. Place a doily over the top of cake and sift confectioners' sugar. Carefully remove the doily. Serve with whipped cream and raspberries.

Strawberry Pie

INGREDIENTS

PASTRY
1 cup flour
1/4 teaspoon salt
6 tablespoons butter
1 egg yolk
2 tablespoons ice cold water

1 cup whipping cream
confectioners' sugar

FILLING
1 1/2 quarts fresh strawberries
1 cup granulated sugar
3 tablespoons cornstarch
1/4 teaspoon salt
1 tablespoon lemon juice
2/3 cup fresh orange juice

INSTRUCTIONS

1. Preheat oven to 425°F. Pastry: add flour, salt, and butter to the bowl of a food processor. Process for a several seconds. Add the egg yolk and water. Process just until dough forms. Shape the dough into a ball and wrap in plastic and refrigerate for 1-2 hours. Roll out pastry to an 11"circle. Line pastry neatly into 9" tart or pie pan. Bake for 12 min. or until golden brown.

2. In a saucepan over medium heat, combine the granulated sugar, cornstarch, salt, lemon juice and orange juice. Bring to a boil, while stirring constantly. Reduce heat to low and cook until it has thickened, approximately 10 minutes total cooking time. Let the glaze cool.

3. Wash, and hull strawberries. Dry completely. Arrange the strawberries in the baked pie shell, placing the pointed ends up. Brush the orange glaze over the strawberries to cover them completely. Refrigerate. When ready to serve, whip the cream and sweeten with a little confectioners' sugar. Cut the pie into wedges and serve with the whipped cream.

Chocolate Ganache Tort

INGREDIENTS

BOTTOM LAYER
5 tablespoons butter
2 tablespoons cocoa powder
1/4 cup brown sugar
3 tablespoons flour
1/4 teaspoon salt
1/2 cup walnuts, chopped fine
2 teaspoons vanilla extract
1 egg

FILLING
1 1/2 cups sliced almonds
4 tablespoons butter

1/4 cup honey
1 cup light brown sugar
1 teaspoon vanilla extract
1 teaspoon fresh lemon juice
1/4 cup heavy cream

FOR GANACHE
1 1/4 cups heavy cream
2 tablespoons sugar
2 tablespoons butter
16 oz. semisweet chocolate, chopped

Fresh or frozen raspberries
3 tablespoons water

INSTRUCTIONS

1. Preheat oven to 350°F. Butter a 9"springform pan. In food processor; place the raspberries and 3 tablespoons water and pulse to make a sauce. Reserve

2. Bottom Layer: Melt butter in a small saucepan and stir in cocoa. Remove pan from heat and add in the sugar stirring to dissolve. Add in flour, salt, chopped walnuts, vanilla and egg. Mix well. Spread batter into the prepared buttered springform pan. Bake 12 minutes. Cool

3. Filling: Sprinkle the sliced almonds over the cooked bottom layer in the springpan. Into a small saucepan; add butter, honey, and brown sugar. Cook over medium heat, stirring occasionally, for 8 minutes. Remove pan from heat. Add vanilla extract, lemon juice, and cream. Blend well. Cool 10 min.. Pour filling evenly over the layer of sliced almonds.

4. Ganache: Heat the heavy cream, sugar, and butter in a large saucepan over medium high heat. Stir constantly, and allow to come to a boil. Put chopped chocolate into a metal bowl and pour hot cream over it. Let stand 5 minutes, then stir until smooth. Cool ganache to room temperature. With an electric mixer, beat just until it holds soft peaks. Spread ganache over filling. Chill cake 5 hours . Transfer cake to a plate Serve with raspberry sauce.

Gingerbread

INGREDIENTS

1 stick butter

1 cup sugar

2 eggs

3/4 cup molasses

3/4 cup boiling water

2 1/2 cups all-purpose flour

2 teaspoon baking soda

1/2 teaspoon salt

1 tablespoon ground ginger

INSTRUCTIONS

1. Preheat oven to 350°F. Butter and flour a 9 inch square pan

2. With an electric mixer at low speed, cream together the butter and sugar, until light. Add the eggs and beat well. Mix together the boiling water and molasses, and blend into the egg-sugar mixture. Add to the bowl; the flour, baking soda, salt and ginger. Stir until combined.

3. Pour the batter into the prepared pan, and bake 35 -40 minutes. Serve warm.

Cherry Cheesecake

INGREDIENTS

CRUST
1/4 cup almonds, toasted
25 chocolate wafer cookies
5 tablespoons butter, softened
1/3 cup sugar
1/2 teaspoon almond extract

TOPPING
3/4 cup dried sour cherries
3/4 cup water
1/4 cup currant jelly
1/4 cup sugar
1 tablespoon lemon juice
1/4 teaspoon almond extract
1 tablespoon cornstarch
2 tablespoons water

FILLING
12 oz. cream cheese
2/3 cup sugar
2 tablespoons cornstarch
1/2 cup sour cream
3 eggs
2 teaspoons vanilla
1 tablespoon lemon juice
fresh mint for garnish

INSTRUCTIONS

1. Preheat oven to 350°F. Butter a 9"springform pan. Crust: In food processor; grind almonds and chocolate wafers., until fine. Add butter, sugar and almond extract. Process until combined. Press crumb mixture evenly onto the bottom and up sides of the springform pan. Bake for 10 min.

2. Topping: In a saucepan over low heat, simmer together the cherries and 3/4 cup water, until the cherries are soft. Add the current jelly, sugar, lemon juice and extract. Mix cornstarch with the 2 tb. water and add to pan. Bring to a boil, stirring constantly until thickened. Cool.

3. Filling: In a bowl with an electric mixer, beat cream cheese, sugar, cornstarch and sour cream until smooth. Beat in eggs, vanilla and lemon juice. Beat well. Pour filling into crust. Bake 50-55 minutes. Cool cake in pan. Spread topping on cake. Refrigerate at least 4 hours. Remove sides of pan and transfer cake to a serving plate. Garnish with fresh mint.

Mango Cheesecake

INGREDIENTS

CRUST
2 cups ground vanilla sandwich
cookies (about 20 cookies)
2 tablespoons butter, softened

TOPPING
1/3 cup apricot preserves
3 tablespoons water
3 tablespoons sugar
1 tablespoon lemon juice

FILLING
12 oz. cream cheese
3/4 cup sugar
2 tablespoons cornstarch
4 eggs
1 teaspoon vanilla
1 tablespoon orange liqueur
1 mango, peeled, seeded, pureed
fresh mint for garnish

INSTRUCTIONS

1. Preheat oven to 350°F. Butter a 9"springform pan. Crust: In food processor; grind up cookies until fine. Add butter, process until combined. Press crumb mixture evenly onto bottom and up sides of the buttered springform pan. Bake 10 minutes. Cool

2. Filling: In a large bowl with an electric mixer, beat cream cheese, sugar, and cornstarch until creamy. Beat in eggs, vanilla, orange liqueur. Beat well. Add the pureed mango. Beat until smooth. Pour filling into crust. Bake 1 hour and then turn off the oven. Allow cheesecake to sit in oven for 15 minutes (with heat off). Remove from oven. Cool cake in pan.

3. Topping: In a saucepan over low heat, simmer together the apricot preserves, water, sugar, and lemon juice. Brush topping on cheesecake.

4 Refrigerate at least 4 hours. Remove sides of pan and transfer cheesecake to a serving plate. Garnish with mint.

Poppy Seed Orange Cake

INGREDIENTS

1 1/2 cups sugar
1/2 cup butter, 1 stick
4 eggs
1 teaspoons vanilla
3/4 cup milk
2 cups flour
2 teaspoons baking powder
1/2 teaspoon baking soda
1/2 teaspoon salt
1/3 cup poppy seeds or 1/4 cup anise seeds

GLAZE
1 cup confectioners' sugar
5 tablespoons butter, melted
2 oranges

INSTRUCTIONS

1. Preheat oven to 325°F. Butter a bundt cake pan . Squeeze the orange juice and reserve. Grate the orange zest and set aside.

2. Using an electric mixer, beat together butter and sugar until creamy. Add in eggs, orange zest, and vanilla. Beat well. Add the milk, flour, baking powder, baking soda and salt. Mix *just* until combined. Fold in poppy seeds. Spoon batter into the prepared bundt cake pan. Bake 50-55 minutes or until skewer inserted comes out clean. Remove from oven.

4. Glaze: Mix together in a saucepan; confectioners' sugar, butter, and 1/2 cup of the reserved orange juice. Cook over medium heat for 6 minutes. Poke holes in the cake with a wooden skewer or fork. Pour glaze over warm cake until all glaze has been absorbed. Invert cake onto plate.

Russian Tea Cakes

INGREDIENTS

1 cup (2 sticks) butter, softened
1/2 cup confectioner's sugar
1 teaspoon vanilla extract
1/4 teaspoon salt
1 tablespoon orange liqueur
1 teaspoon grated orange zest
2 1/4 cups flour
3/4 cup hazelnuts or walnuts, finely chopped
additional confectioner's sugar

INSTRUCTIONS

1. Preheat the oven to 400°F.

2. In a large bowl cream together, using an electric mixer; butter and confections' sugar. Beat until fluffy. Add the vanilla, salt, orange liqueur, orange zest, and mix well. Gradually mix in flour. Stir in chopped nuts.

3. Shape pieces of dough with your hands, and roll into 1"balls. Place onto an ungreased cookie sheet.

4. Bake 12-14 minutes until set (do not brown). Remove from baking sheet. Cool for a few minutes. While still warm, roll in confectioner's sugar to coat. Place on a rack to cool, then roll them once again in the confectioners' sugar.

Shortbread

INGREDIENTS

1/3 cup sugar
1/4 teaspoon salt
2 cups flour
1/2 cup (1 stick) butter
1/4 cup walnuts, finely chopped
1/4 cup chocolate chips, chopped

INSTRUCTIONS

1. Preheat the oven to 325°F. Butter an 8"x 8" square pan.

2. In a mixing bowl; add sugar, salt, and flour. Using your fingers cut in butter, until the mixture resembles coarse meal. Stir in chopped nuts and chopped chocolate.

3. Spread mixture into prepared pan. Press lightly with your hands to flatten the surface of the shortbread.

4. Bake 35-40 minutes until it is a pale golden brown.

5. Cool a few minutes, then cut into fingers. Remove from the pan after it is completely cool. Place onto serving plate.

Coconut Macaroons

INGREDIENTS

2 1/2 shredded coconut, sweetened
1/4 teaspoon salt
1/3 cup flour
1/2 teaspoon baking soda
3/4 cup sweetened condensed milk
2 teaspoons vanilla
1/2 cup almonds, finely chopped
1/2 cup chocolate chips

INSTRUCTIONS

1. Preheat the oven to 350°F. Butter a cookie sheet.

2. In a large mixing bowl; add coconut, salt, flour, and baking soda. Mix together. Add in the condensed milk and vanilla. Stir in chopped nuts and chocolate chips. Stir to combine mixture. Refrigerate for 1 hour.

3. Roll large size balls of the coconut mixture. Place onto a well greased cookie sheet. Should have approximately. 15-18 macaroons.

4. Bake 20 minutes or until macaroons are a golden brown.

5. Remove right away from the cookie sheet. Allow to cool before serving. Arrange macaroons on a serving plate.

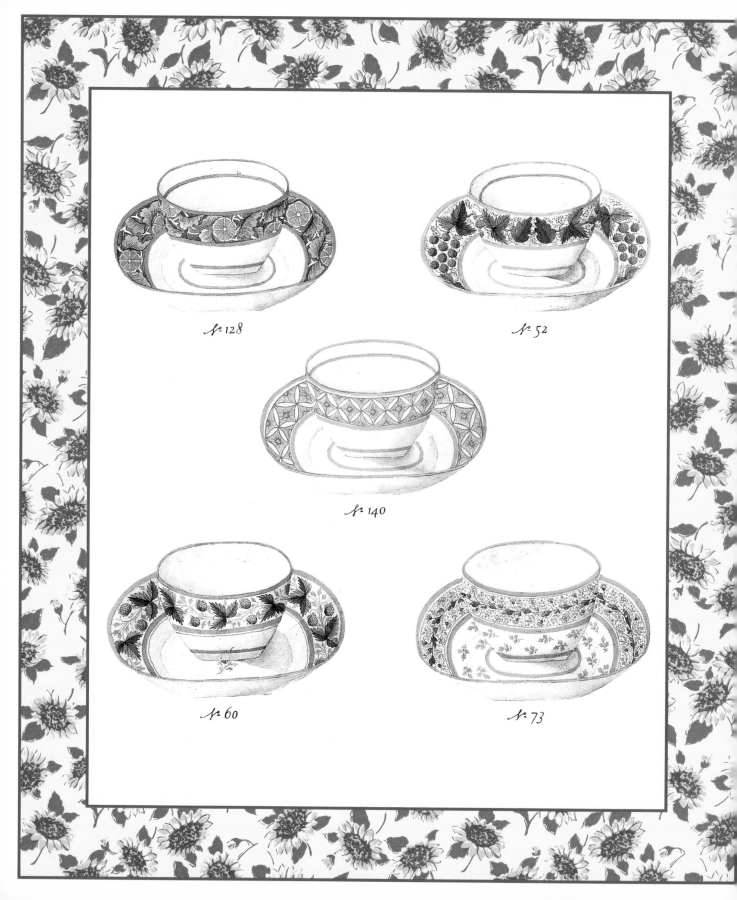

N.° 128

N.° 52

N.° 140

N.° 60

N.° 73

Shortbread Layer Cookies

INGREDIENTS

1 stick butter (1/2 cup), melted
2 cups almond shortbread cookie crumbs
6 oz. pkg. of butterscotch chips
1 cup almonds, chopped
1 1/4 cups shredded coconut, sweetened
14 oz. can of sweetened condensed milk

INSTRUCTIONS

1. Preheat oven to 350°F. Butter a 13 x 9 inch baking pan. Chop the almonds and set aside. Melt the butter. Put the cookies in a food processor and chop them into fine crumbs.

2. Pour the melted butter into the baking pan. Press the cookie crumbs evenly on top of the butter, to make the crust. Sprinkle the nuts over the cookie crumb layer. Next sprinkle the butterscotch chips. Then spread the coconut over the layer of chips. Drizzle the sweetened condensed milk all over the top.

3. Bake 25-28 minutes., until coconut is golden brown. Cool 30 minutes and cut into squares.

Checkerboard Cookies

INGREDIENTS

2 sticks (1 cup) butter or vegetable shortening
2/3 cup sugar
1/8 teaspoon salt
2 teaspoons vanilla extract
2 1/2 cups flour
1 teaspoon baking powder
2 tablespoons cocoa
1 tablespoon chocolate syrup
1 egg white, beaten

INSTRUCTIONS

1. Preheat oven to 350°F. Butter a cookie sheet.

2. Using an electric mixer, beat together butter, sugar and salt until creamy Add in vanilla. Beat well. Add the flour, and baking powder.Mix well.

3. Take 1/2 of the dough and put into a separate bowl. Blend in the cocoa and chocolate syrup into the dough. Mix well and gather the chocolate dough up into a ball and set aside. Take the other half of the dough which is white, and gather the dough up into a ball and also set aside.

4. Take each ball of dough and divide it in two, and roll it with your hands into a log, about 10" long. You will now have 2 white logs and 2 chocolate logs. Brush the tops and sides of the logs with the beaten egg white. Press 1 white log next to 1 chocolate log, and press together, gently. Place the other chocolate log on top of the white log, and place the remaining white log on top of the chocolate log. Gently press together. Wrap in foil and refrigerate for 2 hours. Slice the chilled dough into 1/4"slices, and place onto the greased cookie sheet. Brush tops of cookies with egg white. Bake 10 minutes.

Chocolate Almond Cookies

INGREDIENTS

12 oz. package semisweet chocolate chips
4 tablespoons butter
3 tablespoons brandy
1 teaspoon grated lemon zest
1 cup almonds, ground in food processor
1/8 teaspoon salt
1 cup flour
1 teaspoon baking powder
3 eggs, beaten
1/2 cup sugar
confectioners' sugar

INSTRUCTIONS

1. Preheat oven to 325°F. Butter a cookie sheet.

2. Melt together the chocolate chips and the butter. Add in the brandy and lemon zest. In another bowl; mix together ground almonds, salt, flour, and baking powder. In another bowl, beat together the 1/2 cup sugar and beaten eggs, until light. Add the melted chocolate mixture to the eggs and stir until just combined. Fold in the flour mixture. Refrigerate dough.

3. Roll chilled dough into 1 inch balls. Roll balls in some sugar, then roll the balls in confectioners' sugar. Place cookies onto greased cookie sheet. Bake 12 minutes.

Date Filled Cookies

INGREDIENTS

COOKIES
1 stick (1/2 cup) butter, softened
2 tablespoons molasses
3/4 cup brown sugar
1 teaspoon vanilla extract
1 egg
1/8 teaspoon salt
2 cups flour
1/4 cup bran, natural unprocessed
1 1/2 teaspoon baking powder
1 1/2 teaspoon cinnamon

FILLING
1/2 cup pecans or almonds
1/4 cup brown sugar
juice of 1 orange
8 oz. Medjool Dates, pitted and chopped, about 12 large dates
3 tablespoons water
confectioners' sugar for sifting

INSTRUCTIONS

1. Preheat oven to 375°F. Butter a cookie sheet.

2. Cookies: In a large bowl; beat together the butter, molasses, brown sugar until light and fluffy. Add vanilla and egg. and blend well. Add salt, flour, bran, baking powder, and cinnamon. Beat at low speed *just* until combined. Make dough into a ball and wrap with plastic. Refrigerate

3. Filling: In a food processor; add nuts and chop coarsely. Add 1/4 cup brown sugar, orange juice, chopped dates, & water. Process until thickened.

4. On a lightly floured surface, roll out 1/2 of the chilled cookie dough to 1/8" thick. Keep the remaining half refrigerated. Cut with a round 2 1/2" cookie cutter, dipped in flour. Place rounds onto a greased cookie sheet. Place a teaspoon of filling on each round. Fold half of each round over like a crescent shape. Seal edges. Repeat process for all remaining dough.

5. Bake 10 minutes. Lightly sift confectioners' sugar over tops of cookies. When cool, transfer to serving plate.

Biscotti

INGREDIENTS

1 stick butter (1/2 cup)
3/4 cup sugar
1 tablespoon orange liqueur
1 1/2 teaspoon vanilla extract
1 tablespoon anise seed
1 egg
2 cups flour
1 1/2 teaspoon baking powder
1/4 teaspoon salt
1 cup walnuts or almonds, toasted and chopped
1 egg white

INSTRUCTIONS

1. Preheat oven to 325°F. Butter a baking sheet. Toast and chop nuts.

2. In a large bowl; beat together with an electric mixer; the butter, sugar, orange liqueur, vanilla extract, and anise seed until fluffy. Add the egg and beat until smooth. Using a wooden spoon, add in flour, baking powder, and salt. Stir until combined. Fold in the chopped nuts.

3. Divide the dough into 2 equal pieces. On a lightly floured board, roll each piece with your hands to form a long loaf about 12" long and about 3" wide. Place the 2 loaves onto the greased baking sheet, about 4" apart. Brush tops with beaten egg white. Bake 30 minutes. Transfer loaves to a rack or cutting board to cool.

4. After the loaves are cool, using a serrated knife, slice the loaves on a diagonal into 3/4" thick slices. Place the slices on the greased baking sheet and bake at 300°F. for 15 minutes. Turn off the heat and let the biscotti stay in oven for 20 minutes. Remove from oven and cool completely.

Chocolate Peanut Butter Cookies

INGREDIENTS

COOKIES
1 cup walnuts
6 ounces chocolate chips
1 stick butter (1/2 cup)
1 cup peanut butter
3/4 cup sugar
2 teaspoons vanilla extract
2 eggs
2 1/4 cups flour

1 teaspoon baking powder
1/2 teaspoon baking soda

FROSTING
1 cup confectioners' sugar
1/4 cup brown sugar
2 tablespoons butter
2 tablespoons milk

DRIZZLE
6 oz. semisweet chocolate, melted

INSTRUCTIONS

1. Preheat oven to 325°F. Butter a baking sheet. Toast and chop nuts.

2. Cookies: Melt the chocolate chips over low heat or in the microwave. Set aside. In a large mixing bowl add; the butter, peanut butter and sugar. Beat well with an electric mixer. Add vanilla extract and eggs. Beat until smooth. Beat in melted chocolate. On low speed, add the flour, baking powder, and baking soda. Mix *just* until combined. Fold in the chopped nuts.

3. Divide the dough into 2 equal pieces. On a lightly floured board, roll each piece with your hands to form a log about 12" long and 1 1/2" in diameter. Wrap each roll in plastic and chill for 2 hours.

4. Slice chilled cookie dough into 1/2" slices. Place onto greased cookie sheet. Bake for 16 minutes. Remove from the oven and let cool.

5. Frosting: Blend together confectioners' sugar, brown sugar, butter, and milk. Mix until smooth and creamy. Smooth on a spoonful of frosting on top of each cookie. Then drizzle with the melted chocolate. Use a fork dipped in the melted chocolate and drizzle thin lines of chocolate across the cookies.

Old Fashioned Ginger Snaps

INGREDIENTS

1/2 cup vegetable shortening
1 cup sugar
1 egg
1/3 cup molasses
2 cups flour
2 teaspoons baking soda
2 teaspoons ginger
1 teaspoon cinnamon

INSTRUCTIONS

1. Preheat oven to 350°F. Butter a cookie sheet
2. In a large mixing bowl, using an electric mixer at low speed, cream together the shortening and sugar, until light. Add the egg and molasses and beat well. Stir in the flour, baking soda, ginger and cinnamon. Mix *just* until combined.
3. Roll pieces of dough into small balls. Place onto the greased cookie sheet. Sprinkle tops with a little sugar.
4. Bake 12-14 minutes.

3200

3201

3202

3203

3204

3205

3206

3207

3208

3209

3210

3211

Tea Time Menus

TRADITIONAL LADIES TEA

Goat Cheese & Walnut Tea Sandwiches pg 12
Smoked Salmon Tea Sandwiches, pg 14
Curried Egg Salad Tea Sandwiches, pg 18
Currant Scones, pg 30
Clotted Cream and Jam
Strawberry Tarts, pg 49
Russian Tea Cakes, pg 69
Pot of Tea (your choice)

GENTLEMEN'S TEA

Chicken in Puff Pastry pg 27
Asparagus Gorgonzola Pinwheels, pg. 24
Smoked Turkey & Arugula Tea Sandwiches, 21
Lemon Cream Scones, pg 31
Clotted Cream and Fruit Butter, pg 39
Rum Cake, pg 60
Checkerboard Cookies, pg 74
Pot of Tea/ Glass of Champagne

CHILDREN'S TEA

Cream Cheese & Date Tea Sandwiches pg 17
Curried Egg Salad Tea Sandwiches, pg 18
Smoked Salmon Pinwheels, pg 26
Nut & Raisin Sticky Scones, pg 37
Clotted Cream and Jam
Old Fashioned Ginger Snaps, pg 80
Chocolate Pecan Toffee Bars, pg 53
Pot of Hot Chocolate or Herb Tea

CHOCOLATE LOVER'S TEA

Cream Cheese & Date Tea Sandwiches pg 17
Stilton, Walnut & Pear Tea Sandwiches pg 17
Lemon Cream Scones, pg 31
Clotted Cream and Jam
Chocolate Ganache Tort, pg 63
Almond Butter Bars, pg 55
Chocolate Almond Cookies, pg 75
Pot of Tea (your choice)

Tea Time Menus

VEGETARIAN TEA

Goat Cheese & Walnut Tea Sandwiches pg 12
Chutney & Cheddar Tea Sandwiches pg 13
Minted Radish Tea Sandwiches, pg 20
Currant Scones, pg 30
Lemon Curd, pg 38
Strawberry Pie, pg 62
Coconut Macaroons, pg 71
Pot of Herb Tea (your choice)

THANKSGIVING TEA

Smoked Turkey & Arugula Tea Sandwiches pg 21
Stilton, Walnut, and Pear Tea Sandwiches, pg. 24
Savory Salmon in Filo, pg 28
Cheddar Cornmeal Scones, pg 35
Wendy's Cranberry Tea Bread, pg 43
Clotted Cream and Fruit Butter, pg 39
Cherry Cheesecake, pg 65
Pot of Tea (your choice)

COTTAGE TEA

Rosemary Chicken Salad Tea Sandwiches pg 15
Curried Egg Salad Tea Sandwiches, pg 18
Smoked Salmon Tea Sandwiches, pg 14
Cinnamon Pecan Cream Scones, pg 32
Clotted Cream and Jam
Gingerbread, pg 64
Date Filled Cookies, pg 77
Pot of Tea (your choice)

LATE-NIGHT TEA

Smoked Salmon Tea Sandwiches pg 14
Asparagus Gorgonzola Pinwheels, pg 24
Almond Lemon Tea Bread, pg 40
Fruit Butter, pg 39
Fresh Sliced Fruit
Biscotti, pg78
Pot of Tea (your choice)
Glass of Champagne or Sherry